ELEVATE YOUR STYLE

A COMPREHENSIVE GUIDE TO FASHION MASTERY

KEITH ALLEN HAYES

ELEVATE YOUR STYLE

A COMPREHENSIVE GUIDE TO FASHION MASTERY

KEITH ALLEN HAYES

SBPC

SIMMS BOOKS PUBLISHING CORP.
Publishers Since
Published by Simms Books Publishing Corporation
Jonesboro, GA
Copyright © Keith Allen Hayes, 2024
All rights reserved. No part of this book may be reproduced, scanned, or distributed in any print or electronic form without permission. Please do not participate in or encourage piracy of copyrighted materials in violation of the author's rights. Purchase only authorized editions.
Library of Congress Cataloging in Publication Data

****

Keith Allen Hayes
Elevate Your Style:
A Comprehensive Guide to Fashion Mastery

ISBN:978-1-949433-59-3

Printed in the United States of America
Book Arrangement by Simms Books Publishing
Cover by Mikhail K. Simms

Fashion is not just what you wear; Fashion is understanding what compliments, fits, and makes a statement.

Contents

Chapter 1: Introduction to Fashion 1

Chapter 2: Styles 101 3

Chapter 3: Dos and Don'ts of Fashion 5

Chapter 4: Mastering Color Schemes and Patterns 7

Chapter 5: Crafting the Perfect Look 9

Chapter 6: Matching Shoes with Shirts 11

Chapter 7: Hats, Socks, and Accessories 13

Chapter 8: Decoding Jackets and Blazers 15

Chapter 9: Seasonal Fashion Transitions 17

Chapter 10: Building a Versatile Wardrobe 19

Chapter 1
Introduction to Fashion

In the ever-evolving tapestry of self-expression, fashion stands as a dynamic art form that transcends time. Welcome to the journey of style, where every thread weaves a narrative of identity and creativity. In this chapter, we embark on a discovery of the significance of fashion and the power it holds in shaping one's unique persona.

The Essence of Fashion

Fashion is more than garments; it is a language spoken without words. It encapsulates the spirit of an era, reflects cultural nuances, and empowers individuals to convey their personalities. Understanding this essence is critical to unraveling the profound impact fashion has on our lives.

1.2 The Canvas of Personal Style

At the heart of fashion lies personal style— an ever-evolving canvas upon which individuals paint their tastes, preferences, and moods. From the classic elegance of formal wear to the rebellious vibrancy of street fashion, your style is a signature that echoes your story.

1.3 Navigating the Fashion Landscape

As we delve into the world of fashion, we'll navigate through the myriad of styles, exploring their origins and providing insights into the art of embracing diversity. Fashion is a realm where rules bend, and creativity knows no bounds. It's a journey of self-discovery and empowerment.

A Comprehensive Guide to Fashion Mastery

Prepare to unlock the door to your wardrobe, where each piece is a chapter, and every ensemble tells a tale. Fashion isn't just about what you wear; it's a declaration of who you are. Let's embark on this odyssey, embracing the transformative power of style.

In the ever-evolving tapestry of self-expression, fashion stands as a dynamic art form that transcends time. Welcome to the journey of style, where every thread weaves a narrative of identity and creativity. In this chapter, we embark on a discovery of the significance of fashion and the power it holds in shaping one's unique persona.

A Comprehensive Guide to Fashion Mastery

Chapter 2

Styles 101

In the vast landscape of fashion, styles are the distinct brushstrokes that paint the canvas of self-expression. From the sleek lines of minimalism to the bold strokes of avant-garde, understanding the spectrum of styles is pivotal in crafting a wardrobe that mirrors your essence.

2.1 Exploring Fashion Archetypes

Styles are the archetypes that breathe life into fashion. Dive into casual chic, formal elegance, streetwear edge, and more. Each archetype has its language, telling a unique story and allowing you to choose the dialect that resonates most profoundly with your identity.

2.2 The Art of Style Fusion

Fashion is an ever-evolving art, and the beauty often lies in the fusion of styles. Explore the realms where classic meets contemporary, where street style intertwines with sophistication. The ability to blend styles reflects creativity and showcases a keen understanding of the diverse facets of fashion.

2.3 Discovering Your Signature Style

Amidst the myriad styles lies the quest to discover your signature style. We'll unravel the process of identifying the elements that resonate with you, helping you cultivate a wardrobe that feels authentic. Your signature style is a compass guiding you through the vast sea of fashion choices.

2.4 The Psychology of Style

Fashion is more than aesthetics; it's a psychological dance between the wearer and the world. Delve into the psychology of colors, shapes, and textures. Learn how your style choices impact your perception of self and how others perceive and interact with you.

2.5 The Evolution of Trends

Styles are not static; they evolve with time. Explore

the cyclical nature of trends and how they shape the fashion landscape. Understanding the ebb and flow of trends equips you to make informed choices, blending timeless classics with contemporary flair.

As we journey through the diverse tapestry of styles, remember that fashion is a canvas waiting for your personal touch. Your style is a story; in this chapter, we write it with confidence and flair.

In the vast landscape of fashion, styles are the distinct brushstrokes that paint the canvas of self-expression. From the sleek lines of minimalism to the bold strokes of avant-garde, understanding the spectrum of styles is pivotal in crafting a wardrobe that mirrors your essence.

A Comprehensive Guide to Fashion Mastery

Chapter 3

Dos and Don'ts of Fashion

In the vibrant fashion world, navigating the dos and don'ts is akin to mastering the language of style. This chapter serves as your guide, outlining the principles that elevate your fashion game and cautioning against pitfalls that can dim the brilliance of your sartorial choices.

3.1 The Cardinal Rules

Let's establish the cardinal rules of fashion etiquette. From the importance of fit to the impact of proportion, these rules form the foundation of a polished and put-together look. Understanding and applying these principles will empower you to make style decisions confidently.

3.2 Dressing for Your Body Type

One size fits none in the world of fashion. Discover the art of dressing for your unique body shape, accentuating your strengths, and creating a balanced silhouette. Embrace your body as a canvas, and let your clothing enhance the masterpiece that is you.

3.3 Tailoring and Alterations

well-fitted garment is a game-changer. Uncover the significance of tailoring and alterations as they transform clothing from mere fabric to a bespoke expression of your style. Learn the nuances of alterations that can turn an ordinary outfit into an extraordinary ensemble.

3.4 Accessorizing with Purpose

Accessories are the punctuation marks in the language of fashion. Explore the transformative power of accessories—how a carefully chosen scarf, belt, or statement piece can elevate your look. We'll delve into the art of purposeful accessorizing, ensuring that every work contributes meaningfully to your ensemble.

3.5 Knowing When Less Is More

Simplicity is the ultimate sophistication. Grasp the art

of minimalism and understand when less is more. Overcoming the allure of excess allows your style to shine through with clarity and elegance.

3.6 Breaking the Rules with Intention

While rules guide, creativity often flourishes in breaking them. However, the key lies in intentional rule-breaking. We'll explore instances where bending or breaking the rules can boldly express personal style, adding a touch of rebellion to your sartorial repertoire.

Embark on this journey through the dos and don'ts, and let your style narrative unfold with finesse. Let it be a statement reflecting your confidence and individuality.

A Comprehensive Guide to Fashion Mastery

Chapter 4

Mastering Color Schemes and Patterns

In the kaleidoscope of fashion, color, and patterns, wield the brushes that paint a vivid portrait of personal style. Understanding the intricacies of color theory and the dance of patterns is like mastering the palette, enabling you to craft outfits that resonate with vibrancy and harmony.

4.1 The Color Wheel Unveiled

Embark on a journey through the color wheel—a spectrum of endless possibilities. Learn the emotions and moods associated with each color and discover how to harness this knowledge to convey a visual language through your clothing choices. From the calm embrace of blues to the fiery passion of reds, each hue holds a unique story.

4.2 Harmonizing Color in Outfits

Master the art of harmonizing colors is akin to being

a composer of a symphony. Delve into color schemes, exploring complementary, analogous, and monochromatic palettes. Uncover the secrets of pairing colors that enhance each other and resonate with your style and the mood of the occasion.

4.3 The Impact of Neutrals

Neutrals are the backbone of any wardrobe, providing versatility and sophistication. Understand the power of whites, blacks, grays, and earth tones in creating timeless and chic looks. Discover how neutrals form the canvas upon which you can layer vibrant pops of color or embrace a monochromatic aesthetic.

4.4 Patterns: Artistry in Motion

Patterns add a dynamic layer to your style narrative. From stripes to florals, delve into the world of prints and understand how to incorporate them into your wardrobe with finesse. Learn the art of pattern mixing, creating visually intriguing outfits that showcase your creativity.

4.5 Texture and Dimension

Beyond color and pattern, texture and dimension breathe life into your outfits. Explore the tactile landscape of fabrics and materials, understanding how they contribute to your ensemble's visual and tactile experience. Each texture adds a layer to your fashion story, from the plush warmth of wool to the crisp cotton structure.

4.6 Seasonal Color Palettes

Fashion is a seasonal affair, and color choices often echo the rhythms of nature. Dive into the seasonal color palettes, understanding the harmonized tones with each season. Learn how to adapt your wardrobe to the changing hues of spring blossoms, summer skies, autumn leaves, and winter serenity.

As we unravel the richness of color and patterns, envision your wardrobe as a canvas waiting for your artistic touch. Whether you paint with bold strokes or prefer a subtle watercolor, let your color choices and patterns tell a story uniquely yours.

A Comprehensive Guide to Fashion Mastery

Chapter 5

Crafting the Perfect Look

In fashion, creating a flawless ensemble is an art that goes beyond selecting individual pieces. This chapter is your guide to crafting the perfect look, offering insights into the alchemy of putting together outfits that reflect your personality and resonate with the context of every occasion.

5.1 The Foundation: Fit and Silhouette

The cornerstone of any impeccable look is a well-fitted garment. Understand the nuances of fit and silhouette, appreciating how they contribute to the overall aesthetic. Whether embracing the sleek lines of tailored elegance or the relaxed charm of casual wear, how your clothes fit is the foundation.

5.2 Dressing for Occasions

Every occasion is a stage, and your outfit is the costume that sets the tone. Navigate the nuances of dressing for various occasions, from formal events to casual outings. Uncover the art of striking the perfect balance between standing out and blending in, ensuring that your attire aligns seamlessly with the event's vibe.

5.3 Day-to-Night Transitions

Fashion is dynamic, and your look should be adaptable to different parts of the day. Learn the art of transitioning seamlessly from day to night, understanding how subtle tweaks can elevate your ensemble for evening affairs. From office to cocktails, discover the versatility of a wardrobe that embraces both functionality and style.

5.4 The Power of Statement Pieces

A well-chosen statement piece can transform an outfit from ordinary to extraordinary. Explore the impact of bold accessories, unique garments, or signature items that become the focal point of your look. Master the art of balance, ensuring that statement pieces enhance rather than overpower your overall aesthetic.

5.5 Colors that Reflect Mood

Colors are emotional cues, and incorporating them into your outfit allows you to communicate moods and sentiments. Discover the psychology of color in fashion, choosing hues that align with your spirit and convey the desired message. Let your colors speak, whether radiating confidence in bold red or exuding tranquility in soft blues.

5.6 Building a Capsule Wardrobe

Efficiency meets elegance in the concept of a capsule wardrobe. Explore the art of curating a collection of essential, versatile pieces that form the backbone of your style. A capsule wardrobe simplifies decision-making, ensuring that every item serves a purpose and can be effortlessly mixed and matched.

As you navigate the art of crafting the perfect look, remember that fashion is an expression—a reflection of who you are in a given moment. Each outfit is a chapter, and as you compile them, you weave a narrative that tells the story of your evolving style.

A Comprehensive Guide to Fashion Mastery

Chapter 6

Matching Shoes with Shirts

Footwear is the punctuation mark at the end of the sentence that is your outfit. Understanding the nuances of matching shoes with shirts is an art that contributes significantly to the overall harmony of your look. This chapter delves into the intricacies of pairing shoes with different shirt styles and colors.

6.1 The Foundations of Footwear

Before we explore the realm of matching, let's establish a foundation. Understand the basic types of shoes, from formal to casual, and their roles in different settings. The centerpiece of your attire starts with your shoes, so let's embark on this journey to find the perfect match.

6.2 Formal Elegance: Dress Shoes and Beyond

For formal occasions or professional settings, the choice of footwear matters. Dive into dress shoes, understanding how the color and style should complement your shirt and suit. Beyond the classic Oxford, discover the elegance of loafers, monk straps, and other formal options.

6.3 Casual Chic: Sneakers, Loafers, and More

Casual wear presents a canvas for creativity in footwear. Explore the versatility of sneakers, loafers, boat shoes, and other simple options. Uncover the art of balancing comfort and style, ensuring that your boots harmonize with the color and vibe of your casual shirts.

6.4 Pops of Color and Contrast

Matching doesn't always mean uniformity; sometimes, it's about strategic pops of color or striking contrasts. Learn how to introduce vibrant or contrasting shoes to elevate your outfit. Understand the impact of bold footwear choices in expressing personality and adding visual interest.

6.5 Seasonal Considerations

Just as your wardrobe adapts to the seasons, so should your footwear. Explore the seasonal considerations for matching shoes with shirts. From the warmth of boots in winter to the breathability of loafers in summer, align your shoe choices with the climate and occasion.

6.6 Sneakers and Smart Pairing

Sneakers have evolved beyond the gym to become a casual and semi-formal staple. Uncover the art of pairing sneakers with shirts, mastering the delicate balance between athleisure and smart casual. Sneakers offer a spectrum of possibilities, whether embracing monochromatic looks or experimenting with patterns.

As you navigate the labyrinth of footwear, remember that the right pair of shoes doesn't just complete your outfit; it amplifies your style statement. Let your footwear be the exclamation point that emphasizes your fashion narrative.

A Comprehensive Guide to Fashion Mastery

Chapter 7

Hats, Socks, and Accessories

Accessories are the punctuation marks that add flair and personality to your fashion story. This chapter explores the art of adorning yourself with hats, socks, and accessories, showcasing how these elements can elevate your style from ordinary to extraordinary.

7.1 The Crown of Style: Hats Unveiled

Hats are not merely coverings; they are statements. Explore the world of hats, from the classic fedora to the casual beanie. Understand style nuances and how to incorporate them into your outfits to enhance your overall aesthetic. Unveil the transformative power of a well-chosen hat.

7.2 Sock Sophistication: A Peek Underneath

Often overlooked but never to be underestimated, socks are the unsung heroes of fashion. Delve into the art of sock selection, understanding how colors, patterns, and lengths contribute to your overall look. Whether making a bold statement or harmonizing with your ensemble, socks deserve their moment in the spotlight.

7.3 The Language of Ties and Scarves

Neckties and scarves are the storytellers at the neckline. Uncover the intricacies of tying knots and draping scarves, exploring the visual and symbolic impact these accessories bring. Let your neckwear speak volumes, whether conveying professionalism with a Windsor knot or adding a bohemian flair with a silk scarf.

7.4 Belts as Anchors and Accents

Beyond their functional role, belts serve as anchors defining your waistline and accents punctuating your style. Learn to choose a belt that complements your outfits, exploring various materials, colors, and buckle styles. Discover the transformative power of a well-chosen belt in refining your silhouette.

7.5 Statement Jewelry and Watches

Jewelry and watches are the finishing touches that exude refinement. From the elegance of a wristwatch to the boldness of statement jewelry, explore how these accessories can convey sophistication and individuality. Learn the art of layering jewelry and selecting timepieces that align with your style aesthetic.

7.6 Bags and Beyond Carrying Style

Your bag is more than a functional accessory; it's a style statement. Delve into the world of bags, from briefcases to backpacks, understanding how form meets function in carrying style. Explore how the right bag can complement your outfit, serving as both practical and fashionable.

As you embrace the world of hats, socks, and accessories, remember that every detail contributes to the symphony of your style. Let these elements be the notes that compose a melody uniquely yours, resonating with confidence and individuality.

A Comprehensive Guide to Fashion Mastery

Chapter 8

Decoding Jackets and Blazers

Jackets and blazers are the protagonists in the drama of outerwear, adding layers of sophistication and style to your wardrobe. In this chapter, we decode the intricacies of different outerwear options, offering insights into styling, occasions, and how to seamlessly integrate them into your fashion repertoire.

8.1 The Versatility of Jackets

Jackets come in various styles, each offering a unique flair. From the classic denim jacket to the rugged leather biker jacket, understand how different materials and designs contribute to the overall vibe of your outfit. Discover the art of selecting jackets that harmonize with your style and the occasion.

8.2 Blazers: Elegance Redefined

Blazers are the epitome of refined style. Explore the nuances of blazers, from classic single-breasted to more daring double-breasted options. Uncover the elegance of lapels, buttons, and fabrics, understanding how to choose a blazer that complements your physique and aligns with the formality of the setting.

8.3 Suiting Up with Confidence

Suits are the epitome of sartorial sophistication. Delve into the world of suits, understanding the elements of a well-fitted ensemble—from the jacket and trousers to the shirt and tie. Whether navigating a formal event or making a statement in a stylish casual suit, suiting up is an art that requires attention to detail.

8.4 Casual Blazers: Bridging Formality and Comfort

Casual blazers offer a versatile middle ground between formality and comfort. Explore how to pair them with different shirt styles, creating looks seamlessly transitioning from day to night. Discover the art of layering with casual blazers, adding dimension to your outfit while maintaining a relaxed aesthetic.

8.5 Outerwear for Every Season

As the seasons change, so should your outerwear. Explore the outerwear options suitable for different weather conditions, from lightweight bomber jackets in spring to insulated parkas in winter. Master the art of layering, ensuring that your outerwear not only shields you from the elements but also enhances your style.

8.6 Accessories that Complement Outerwear

The right accessories can amplify the impact of your outerwear. Explore how scarves, gloves, and hats can seamlessly integrate with jackets and blazers to create a cohesive and stylish look. Uncover the art of accessorizing outerwear for both practicality and visual appeal.

As you navigate the realm of jackets and blazers, remember that outerwear is not just a shield against the elements—it's an opportunity to showcase your style with confidence and finesse. Let your jackets and blazers be the outer layer that completes the visual symphony of your ensemble.

A Comprehensive Guide to Fashion Mastery

Chapter 9

Seasonal Fashion Transitions

In the ever-changing tapestry of fashion, adapting your style to the seasons is a practical consideration and a stylistic opportunity. Chapter 9 explores the nuances of seasonal fashion transitions, guiding you through wardrobe adjustments that harmonize with the rhythms of nature.

9.1 Wardrobe Essentials for Every Season

Each season brings its own set of wardrobe essentials. Dive into the must-haves for spring's blossoms, the breezy attire for summer, the warm layers for autumn, and the cozy ensembles for winter. Understand how selecting season-specific essentials ensures that your wardrobe is both functional and fashionable.

9.2 Color Palette Evolution

Just as nature transforms with each season, so should your color palette. Explore the hues that resonate with spring's freshness, the vibrant tones of summer, the earthy and warm shades of autumn, and the cool, muted winter colors. Learn how adapting your color choices adds a touch of seasonality to your style.

9.3 Fabric Matters: Navigating Seasonal Textures

Fabrics play a pivotal role in seasonal comfort and style. From the breathability of cotton in summer to the warmth of wool in winter, understand how to select fabrics that align with the climate. Discover the art of layering with lightweight materials in warmer months and embracing cozy textiles when temperatures drop.

9.4 Footwear for Every Weather

Your choice of footwear should be as adaptable as the weather. Explore the range of shoes suitable for each season, from breathable summer sandals to waterproof winter boots. Uncover the art of maintaining style and functionality in your shoe choices as you traverse the seasons.

9.5 Transitioning Pieces: Bridging the Seasons

Transitional pieces are the bridge between seasons, allowing you to navigate the changing climate seamlessly. Explore the versatility of lightweight jackets, layering sweaters, and versatile accessories that effortlessly transition your wardrobe from one season to the next.

9.6 Mindful Wardrobe Rotation

As the seasons shift, so should your wardrobe. Embrace the practice of a mindful wardrobe rotation, stowing away off-season items while bringing forward those suited for the current climate. Learn the art of decluttering and organizing to ensure your wardrobe remains functional and inspiring. As you embark on the journey of seasonal fashion transitions, remember that adapting your style to nature's cycles is not just practical—it's an opportunity to showcase your fashion versatility. Let each season be a chapter in the evolving story of your style, and with thoughtful transitions, you'll navigate the year with flair and finesse.

A Comprehensive Guide to Fashion Mastery

Chapter 10

Building a Versatile Wardrobe

In the grand symphony of fashion, a versatile wardrobe is the conductor that orchestrates a harmonious ensemble for every occasion. Chapter 10 explores the art of building a timeless, adaptable wardrobe and a true reflection of your unique style identity.

10.1 Essentials for Every Wardrobe

A versatile wardrobe begins with a foundation of essentials. Explore the timeless pieces that form the backbone of your closet—crisp white shirts, well-fitted jeans, a classic blazer, and the little black dress. Understand how these essentials serve as the canvas upon which you can build many looks.

10.2 Quality over Quantity

The mantra of a versatile wardrobe is quality over quantity. Learn the art of discerning craftsmanship and selecting pieces that stand the test of time. Discover how investing in well-made, durable items enhances your style and contributes to sustainable and mindful fashion.

10.3 Mix and Match Mastery

The magic of a versatile wardrobe lies in the ability to mix and match effortlessly. Explore the art of pairing different pieces to create a variety of looks. Learn how strategic combinations can take your wardrobe from day to night, from casual to formal, ensuring that each item plays multiple roles.

10.4 Capsule Wardrobe Wisdom

Consider the concept of a capsule wardrobe—a curated collection of versatile pieces that effortlessly work together. Delve into crafting a capsule wardrobe for different occasions, ensuring each item serves a purpose and matches up with various ensembles.

10.5 Trends with a Timeless Twist

While trends come and go, infusing a touch of current styles into your wardrobe can add a contemporary flair. Discover the art of incorporating trend-conscious pieces in a way that aligns with your style without compromising your wardrobe's timeless essence.

10.6 Wardrobe Maintenance and Mindful Shopping

Building a versatile wardrobe is an ongoing journey requiring maintenance and mindful additions. Explore the art of wardrobe curation, understanding when to declutter, repair, or invest in new pieces. Learn the importance of conscious shopping choices that align with your style narrative and values.

As you embark on the endeavor of building a versatile wardrobe, envision it as a collection of stories to be told. Each piece is a character, and together, they create a narrative that evolves with you. With the principles of essentials, quality, mix-and-match mastery, capsule wardrobe wisdom, and mindful shopping, your wardrobe becomes a timeless reflection of your style journey.

www.ingramcontent.com/pod-product-compliance
Lightning Source LLC
Chambersburg PA
CBHW021002090426
42736CB00010B/1428

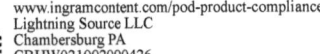